Meta-tations

A Book of Mental Meanderings

by Jerry L. Curtis, Ph.D.

Robbie Dean Press
Ann Arbor, MI

Cover Design by John Meszaro

Copyright © 2005

All rights reserved. No part of this book may be reproduced or transmitted in any form or by any means, electronic or mechanical, including photocopying and recording, or by an information retrieval system, without permission in written form by the publisher.

ISBN: 1-889743-41-0

CONTENTS

INTRODUCTION	iv
ABOUT ART	1
CHANGE	9
EARTH	19
HUMOR	25
ILLUSION	33
LOVE	43
ME & THEE	49
OCCIDENTALISMS	57
ORIENTALISMS	65

INTRODUCTION

The art of meta-tating is really far more common than the reader may imagine. Like sex, it goes on behind the barriers built around it and is rarely discussed with any degree of accuracy.

This book is nothing more or less than a short collection of epiphanal thoughts that follow no set pattern and are not a monopoly of the schooled or the elite. A plumber is as likely to think great thoughts as the statesman or the philosopher; he just makes less of a fuss about them.

Still, it is perhaps unfortunate that such flashes of thought are so seldom conveyed to others, since they represent the common means of communication we humans possess: our humor, our frustrations, our silent joys, and our despair.

The style of these *Meta-tations* is as simple as the flow of thought itself. The readers will realize, as they thumb through this collection of aphorisms, that many of them have passed through their own consciousness at some remote point in time. What follows, then, is an expression of ideas and emotions as much yours as mine. If they make you smile, my ambitions will be fulfilled.

— JLC

ABOUT ART

The Trouble with Telling Stories . . .

I tell stories . . .
not knowing
whether the listener
believes them
or not
And not knowing
whether the things told
are true
or not
And through it all
knowing only
that the stories
must be told

Canvassing for Art

Too many artists of our generation
have neither skill nor imagination
But, with listening fingers
they have mass-produced
an investor's paradise
of "What's it?" objects
that are, admittedly,
conversation pieces
but that do not reach out
to the soul.

To my mind
there is not much art
in the modern practice
of canvassing

Sensing Music

Music is one of the most
soothing of activities because it
appeals to the sense of touch
as well as to the sense of hearing
There is a physical awareness
of its harmony
that affects the ears

But there is also recognition
of a sort of buzzing
of the whole body
that results from the coordinated
fusion of harmonious notes
So music reaches its Satori
in the sense of touch

The Potter's Foot

The potter's foot
can be as important
in the creative process
as his hands

But who praises
the foot?

Moving from Bar to Bar

Thirty-two bars
should be enough
to intoxicate
any music-lover

The Bare Truth

To discover, uncover,
lay bare,
denude,
or strip
is —
on all levels —
one of the most exciting
and rewarding
of human endeavors

Ce qui est essentiel . . .

Language
is such a poor substitute
for communication

CHANGE

The Cerebral Compass

Life's real tragedies
are those possibilities
that people don't have
the courage
to explore
Because unexplored possibilities
are like unsung songs,
unread books,
and untried love:
not always well sung
or bearing a good plot
or sweet fulfillment;
but impossible to know
if not explored

The Eternal Round

On the horizon
(the contemplator looks out of himself)
are fleeting shadows
of a changing world —
the End
and the Beginning
of the Eternal Round
But in my mirror
is an image
of life's stability
that, in tomorrow's
looking glass
will be the same face —
except for a gray hair
or two

Cross-currents

The tides of life
are fairly predictable
It is life's cross-currents
that disarm and frighten us
Because
they come without warning
And because
they carry us
willing or unwilling
to unknown places

Moving On

I am migrating from here to there
Unhappy at having to leave
Unsure of where I am going
But aware
that hidden wheels turn
and unseen forces move,
that I dance, move, turn, and feel
and that I must flow with the times,
that I must adapt if I am to survive
Or else I can stay here
to etiolate and fade away
But if I do
my soul will go on without me
So
I am migrating

The Shrinking Planet

The wandering merchant of today
dressed in a three-piece suit
carries his wares
in a combination-locked
briefcase
taking to remote places
via sonic booms and banter
the new mousetrap

Concretization of Métaphore

It is ironic
that the substantive: WATCH
derives from a verb
designating what is now
a lost art
We watch a watch
We no longer simply watch
If we knew how to watch
we wouldn't need a WATCH
Primitive man had his subtleties
He was a watcher
Or, in today's jargon
he was a WATCH
He marked his own time

Metamorphosis

Metamorphosis
is not unique to butterflies
For men, too
are creatures of change
But unlike the lowly larva
we do not weave our own cocoons
but are captured by silken threads
of seductive weavers
of propaganda,
held fast in the grip of ideas
alien to us
and
if this is not enough
we can emerge from the chrysalis state
and have a transplant

Regeneration

Tides
are cursing through my brain
carrying hope to forgotten places
rushing through my veins
watching me decay
yet bringing new life
renewing my soul

All cross-currents
of breath and blood
All pulsating thoughts
of regeneration

Passive/Aggressive

Each day of this life
we are faced with the choice
of floating on the waves
surfing with life's flow
or swimming
against the current
to the other shore

EARTH

Terrestrial Wisdom

The earth has learned
long ago
to accept the fact
that the sun
can warm it
only half at a time

The Stormy Petrel

I would like to be
like the wind.
When it passes
Nature quivers
then regains its poise
Leaves shudder
then stay still
Birds stop their wings
and soar
on its hidden momentum
It comes
All is touched
Then it is gone

The Furrowed Brow

Adrenaline to the muscles
Blood to the brain
Air to the lungs
Food to the mouth
One hand to another
The cycle of living goes on
And the correlations
renew themselves
The ruts run deep in the road
long after the rain has ceased
And man's responsibility to man
emerges anew
after each death of an ideology
after violence descends like rain

Cosmos vs Chaos

The threadbare stupidity
of the human creature
is manifest
not in the discovery
but in the misuse of
the wonders of our earth and minds
We have not yet adapted
to our planet
convinced that it
must adapt to us

We likewise attempt
to order our minds
rather than to allow our minds
to order us

Landfill

Vertical landscapes
of steel and blocks and glass
have caged my soul
atrophied my spirit
and blunted my senses
Is there earth beneath my feet?

HUMOR

Out On A Limb

A reminder to modern man:
The five-pronged
L-shaped
projections
at the lower extremity
of the human body
can be used
to propel that mass
from place to place
in cases
of extreme emergency

Nature/Nourish

I don't mind
leaving things to Fate
if
once in awhile
I can give Fate
a kick in the ass

The Ultimate Mariology

Queen, save the God!

Mixed Messages

Action speaks
But it often says the opposite
to what it means

Forces vives

Superman
got his energy
from krypton
My watch runs
on quartz
And that computer
on silicon
So what makes me tick?

The Arianic Law

In the waking state
the only real inconvenience
is that the body
must perform
according to
the cerebral script

Multiple Choice

The end is in
- ☐ sight
- ☐ hearing
- ☐ taste
- ☐ touch
- ☐ smell

ILLUSION

The Burden of Reality

Illusion
plays such a dominant role
in the human comedy
that most of us
cannot distinguish it
from reality

And even if we were capable
of such a display of
perception
few of us
could live with the burden
of our discoveries

The Fleeting Image

Man feeds upon the familiar
In the familiar
he places all his human confidence
But what seems familiar to us
is really an illusion.
Is that me
in the reflecting glass
or a mere image of me?
Can I really see
my true self
with my own eyes?
Or can I trust
my reflective thoughts?
How can I hope to know
anything with certainty?

The Business of Our Intentions

Our journey through this life
is like a white ribbon
in the sky
Stirred into celestial froth
by the business
of our intentions
Only to disintegrate
into thin air
Or to join the clouds
with the passing
of time

Thus we make our mark

Splintered Identity

Our earthly trajectory
is like that of a raindrop:
a hazy origin
a precipitous path
and an end
that splinters
our self-contained identity
into smithereens

Star-Gazers

Today
people consult the stars
according to Ptolemaic standards
And draw conclusions
unworthy of Copernicus

The star you are wishing upon
may have burned out
eons ago

Why do humans seek
so diligently
to be determined
in their various lives
by external forces?

Today's Pterodactyl

Today
I saw
a silver-skinned bird
swallow
three hundred people
and
carry them off

Here and Now

Ripples
in an ocean of thought
carried along in the
maelstrom of events
that make up one life

Not knowing where
they are going
but aware of where
they have been
and where they are

The Seventh Veil

Behind the seventh veil
I also discovered
the sound of laughter
And am now deciding
whether I, too, shall laugh
Or whether
I shall find he who laughs
and destroy him

Lost Eden

The world of my infancy
was an enormous womb
peaceful and warm

Eden was my garden
The sun shone for me

And even today
I have not yet
fully recovered
from this deception

LOVE

Does It Make Sense?

I don't know
if I agree
with
your definition of love
But
I'll believe it
when I feel it

Shortfall

Human relations are based
on expectations
that are never
fully voiced
fully understood
or fully carried out

The Two-Fold "We"

The most precious aspect
of any relationship
is the area
that is inviolable
by others

The Dark Side

Like the moon
each of us has a dark side
a part of us
mysterious and unknown
that we keep to ourselves
and that
once in awhile
is glimpsed
by a privileged explorer
who cares to know
what we are really like
inside and out

Freedom vs Commitment

The basic problem
of allowing for more freedom
than mutual commitment
in the relationship
between Man and Woman
is the inevitable conclusion
that you can do without
one another

What are your needs?
And without them
what is the point
on any relationship?

ME & THEE

Separate Realities

Apparently
it is unrealistic to expect
other creatures
who use another brain
to form their vision
of the world
and another body
to feel it —
To see things
my way
or feel them
as I do

Agreeing to Disagree

The great difficulty with
objecting to other people's ideas
is that one is viewed
as a burster of bubbles
or a destroyer of dolls' houses

Along with this
one is accused of being egotistical
even when (or if)
one discerns
the discrepancies
present in the views of others
Even admitting
to one's own uncertainties
does not seem to atone
in the minds of others
for the crime
of pointing out theirs

The Search for Individuality

Life's most fearsome struggle
is to tear one's self and soul
away from bourgeois (non-thinking)
conventionality

The next most fearsome struggle
is to survive in a society
of bourgeois conventions

The next most fearsome struggle
is to resist the impulsion
to conventionalize
anti-bourgeois sentiments

The next most awesome struggle
is to avoid
dying of solitude

Thinking About Thinking

This generation
speaks of mind-expansion
as if it understood
the mind

If we were more modest
we would say
of our generation
that we have begun to think
about thinking
and leave expanding the mind
to some future clan
more advanced than ourselves

Security vs Freedom

How do we reconcile
in our dealing with others
our mutually exclusive needs
for security and freedom?

Aim for freedom
and you are accused of being
a libertine

Search for security
and you are regarded as a
naive idealist

Avoid both
and you are categorized as
an escapist

The Cost of Freedom

Since no one is free
except
at the expense of someone else,
please put my freedom
on your account

Sept cent millions de Chinois . . .

Life's greatest quest

is

for me-dom

OCCIDENTALISMS

Escape from the Self

In the Occident
we have coddled our brains
with the bombardment of
possibilities for
leisure-time activities
The world comes to our doorstep
to entertain us
And in the process we have
developed an aversion
to being alone
face-to-face
with our own thoughts

Evasion has become
a collective way of life

Power and the People

If we lived
at the concentric center
of the Great Design
we'd understand power
and its emissions
that spiral out
touching all things
and all people

The only trouble is
that there are
so many great designs

Vaporous Truth

Truth goes up in vapors
and rains down
in someother place
at someother time
for someother one

Freedom and the Unabsolute

True freedom begins
with an individual's detachment
from so-called
Immutable laws

The Individual vs the Collectivity

The fact
that we are all
Individuals
is a truth
that negates
all collective notions
of truth

A Matter of Mind

Religion
for some
is an incidental severing
of the synaptic vesicles

It anaesthetizes
against suffering
if the mind
concedes

The Dialectic of Opposites

From place to sacred place
we move in gentle confusion
basking in warm sun
or stepping between the rubble
filling our lungs with clean air
or coughing back the fumes
catching the hazy purple
of the fly's wing
or catching his disease
loving and knowing
love's pain
moving through life's days
looking and feeling
and forever wondering

ORIENTALISMS

The Silent Language

The Oriental silence
has
so much to say

The True Path

It is possible
that if we are ever searching
and never reaching the truth
that the searching
is the truth
Because truth
is not necessarily
at the end of the quest
or at the mountain's top
but may as well be
along the way
or even the way itself

The House of Saud

Ramadan—
the holy month of fasting—
begins tonight
at moonrise

But many Saudis
won't see the rising moon
because
they have oil
in their eyes

Fatality

Feeling helpless
to control one's destiny
is a Western notion that
in the East
is a state of being

Fork and Finger

Tonight, a silver fork
Tonight, a regal repast
with linen napkins
and sonorous crystal
Tomorrow
squatting with my friends
my hand in the common pot
I watch and live
the changes
of a culture
transforming
from old to new
in a perpetual state
of becoming

Digression on Digestion

Eating an egg
is not as magical
as laying one

The Golden Mean

Finding a true balance
in living
is like
cracking a walnut
with a sledgehammer

Earth-Bound

An airport
is a prison
locking in those
who stay behind

His-story

We are merely
Once
Upon a time

Paradise Lost

Nothing
can ever be said
to accurately describe
what didn't happen

Reconciliation

True flights of the mind
should be round trips
because
traveling is nice
but so is coming home

The Closed Mind

Hermetical systems
are not open
to criticism

Quiet, please!

I cannot really hear myself
unless I silence
the world around me

Haiku

Even the low worm
invokes eternal oneness
Circles meaning life

Visual Reality

The eye
is both the mirror
of the soul
and the periscope
that peeps into
the universe
bringing together
into the cerebral mixer
the fixed
and that
which moves

Non-Meeting of Minds

I have been accused
of self-deception
because I did not agree
with the conception
of another Self

Problems of Proliferation

The same India
that cannot feed her people
is feverishly preparing
nuclear bombs
that can destroy
all her people

Should they fear the foreigner
or themselves?

Gardens Wherein Oil Flows

The Bedouin has raised his tent
and as he looks towards Mecca
hordes of men throng to him
coming from the green fields
coming from the gardens wherein rivers flow
coming from Europe and the East
to share with him a drink of his black oil
while he
as in times past
sips his coffee and wonders
as the Shamaal blows
and the desert crescent
sheds its light
Why these pilgrims
have come to him

Desert Quest

Once the Arab mind
conceived pyramidal thoughts

But now
the linear conceptions
have miraged
into a Bedouin's path

The End of the Road

Roads do end
but they always lead
somewhere

So if you continue
on the road you've taken
You will arrive
at that road's end,
at that somewhere
your feet are taking you,
unless you change directions
and take another path
to anotherplace

Mindpower

Change and survival
take place
between the ears